Fa lee-lee chirren ebrywhey wa need fa laarn ta respec dey eldas.
Gullah

For little children everywhere who need to learn to respect their elders.
English

Little MUDDY WATERS

To Zoe &
Audrey !

Ronald Daise

A Gullah Folk Tale by Ronald Daise

Illustrated by Barbara McArtor

G.O.G. Enterprises   Beaufort, South Carolina

Published by G.O.G. Enterprises, Beaufort, South Carolina

Text ©1997 by Ronald Daise
Illustrations © 1997 by Barbara McArtor
Foreword ©1997 by Eleanora E. Tate

Design by Melinda Smith Monk

MUDDY WATERS™ is a trademark of the Estate of McKinley Morganfield (aka
'Muddy Waters') and used by Ron and Natalie Daise, dba G.O.G. Enterprises
under authorization.

First Edition

Library of Congress Catalog Card Number: 97-80693
ISBN: I-891503-01-4

Printed in the United States of America

Author's Note

In the Gullah tradition, as in West African heritage, children are given "basket names," or nicknames, at birth. Basket names reflect physical features or actions or activities surrounding the birth. For instance, "Little Big Eyes," "Trumpet Player," or "Summer Breeze" could be basket names given to children who are bright-eyed or who cry loudly or who are born on a peaceful summer day.

Little Muddy Waters was so named because of his pretty, dark complexion. My real-life cousin was called Muddy Waters because the midwife had to cross a muddy river to attend his delivery. He was the grandson of Miss Freeze, who had been born on a very cold day.

The story of Little Muddy Waters is not based on the life of the legendary blues singer Muddy Waters. I respectfully thank the Estate of McKinley Morganfield (aka 'Muddy Waters') for granting license to use the name.

I extend a special thank you to Barbara McArtor, whose vision of Little Muddy Waters as a storybook preceded my wife's and mine; my heartfelt appreciation to Fairl Zurbuchen for assuring my wife and me that dreams are attainable; and my gratitude to Barbara Carter and Carol Tuynman, whose editorial direction helped me to transform a told tale into a written one.

Foreword

by Eleanora E. Tate

When Gullah storyteller Ronald Daise published *De Gullah Storybook*, his classic counting book for children in 1989, readers were introduced to the richness of the Gullah language. Now in Daise's new book *Little Muddy Waters*, we are introduced to a hardheaded boy's loving family and to other lively Gullah-speaking residents who live on St. Helena, a coastal South Carolina Sea Island near Beaufort.

In this book, Daise, who was born on St. Helena Island, recounts the story of what happens when young Little Muddy Waters learns the hard way that adults—parents, grandparents and other old folks—have valid reasons for insisting that children "respect yo elders and do what's right."

The book's down-home beliefs—a bag of sulfur and garlic worn around the neck keeps away mean spirits; Spanish moss placed in the shoe helps bring down one's high blood pressure; oil bush plant leaves placed on the chest help rid one of fever—illustrate coastal South Carolina home remedies that were readily available when doctors were not.

The Gullah language is said to have originated centuries ago among enslaved persons brought from the continent of Africa and from the Caribbean to southeastern coastal states like South Carolina and Georgia and their barrier islands (Sea Islands like St. Helena, Daufuskie and Hilton Head). Though these persons were born in a variety of West African kingdoms, they wisely mixed colonial English (and other European languages) with their own and created a common language—Gullah—as a means of communicating with each other.

The Gullah way of life and its traditions survived into the twentieth century particularly in homes located on the Sea Islands, but the past quarter century has seen a decline in Gullah lifestyles as children on the Sea Islands and in surrounding areas move away from their roots.

Lately, though, there has been a revival of interest in Gullah. Many coastal residents, like author Daise and his wife Natalie, an accomplished storyteller in her own right, still proudly celebrate the Gullah heritage, still speak the language, and preserve its songs, idioms, stories and values.

Daise combines the tales of "Raw Head and Bloody Bones" and "Little Eight John" to create *Little Muddy Waters*, a lighthearted, informative story that should entertain and satisfy readers of all ages.

Now Little Muddy Waters was one good looking, dark-skinned boy. He was dark and dashing just like an African prince. Little Muddy Waters was good looking just like all the other dark-skinned boys on St. Helena Island. But there was something just a little bit different about him. That boy was—now, there's no other way to say it—HARDHEADED! He got into everything. And he did everything that he was told not to do.

Grandma Waters tried to teach him all the things that he should know. She wanted him to be a good little boy. And she taught him to mind his manners. But Little Muddy Waters thought most things his grandma told him were the funniest things he had ever heard. He would just laugh and laugh and laugh.

It was getting more and more difficult for Grandma and Big Papa Waters to raise such a don't-listen-to-anybody, do-whatever-he-wanted-to-do little child. And they weren't just raising Little Muddy Waters, either. They also kept his older sister and his younger brother.

"Respect yo elders and do what's right," Grandma would tell them. "And don't comb your hair outdoors. No, no, no, now. If you do, birds will get it. And if a bird gets your hair and makes a nest with it, you'll get headaches. Real bad headaches."

Little Muddy Waters just laughed at his grandma's words. Then he said politely, "Why, no Mahm. I won't comb my hair outdoors."

And he told the truth. He did not comb his hair outdoors. But what he did do was take his grandma's hair out of the trash can. She had pulled the loose hairs out of her comb and nicely rolled them up inside some tissue paper. He carried that ball of hair into the woods. And then he dropped it right in the middle of a bird's nest.

When the Mama Bird started making a nest with that old woman's hair,
Grandma Waters got a headache so-o-o-o-o bad, she fainted. Little Muddy
Waters came home and saw his grandma holding her head. "That bird
must have been building a nest fa true," he thought. And then he just
laughed and laughed.

"Respect yo elders and do what's right," Grandma Waters said. "Don't laugh at people when you see they're hurt. Uh-uh! You gon rememba what I say?"

Before Grandma Waters finished talking, Little Muddy Waters' sister walked in and put a wet towel on the old woman's head. His brother started fanning Grandma with a folded newspaper. Little Muddy Waters, however, looked on silently for a few minutes. He never answered his grandma. He just walked away.

A few days later when Grandma Waters was feeling better, she found Little Muddy Waters and pulled him aside.

"Respect yo elders and do what's right," she said. "Now, listen to me good. Don't you walk out of someone's house from a different door than the one you came in. Or you'll bring a heapa bad luck on that family."

As soon as his grandma was out of sight, Little Muddy Waters crept out the front door. He turned right around and ran straight through that house. And right on out the back door. And this was his own home!

Did bad luck strike! Little Muddy Waters' sister was cooking in the kitchen when she accidentally cut herself. In two places! With the butcher knife!

Now Big Papa knew exactly what to do. He pulled down some spider webs from a corner of the kitchen ceiling. He pushed them inside one of those cuts. The other was a little bit deeper, though. So Big Papa made a mixture of some mashed up soap and sugar and pushed it inside. And the bleeding stopped. Just like he knew it would.

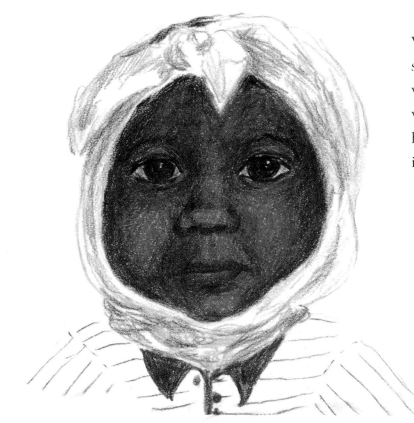

But that was not all the bad luck that had come on that family. Uh-uh. Little Muddy Waters' brother got the mumps. His throat was sticky, sore, swollen and painful! And on top of that, he got a fever so high, the boy was just about delirious.

Was he a sight! His grandparents had laid some salted pork skin on a strip of cloth. The meat was resting against his throat. And the cloth was tied atop his head. Big Papa told him he had to walk around like that until the swelling in his throat went down.

When he got the high fever, Big Papa went out
into the woods looking for something—the oil
bush plant. He found it and brought home
some of those wide, green leaves. He lay them
on the little boy's chest and thighs. Grandma
Waters gave him some lifeverlasting tea with
honey. Then she sent him to bed. She
wrapped him up under five heavy homemade
quilts to sweat that fever out.

Grandma Waters started worrying. She worried about her sick grandson. She watched her granddaughter's hand heal. And she worried about how such an accident could've happened to a child who was always so careful. She wondered if someone had done something to bring all this bad luck and misery on the family.

Everybody said, "No," except Little Muddy Waters. Now he knew something about everything that had happened. But he didn't say a word about anything. To anybody. He didn't even act sorry about anything. Uh-uh-uh.

One day, soon after that, Grandma Waters was at her wits' end. About Little Muddy Waters' silence whenever she asked questions. About how he always showed up soon after something bad had happened. About how that boy was always laughing when others felt sad. And always laughing whenever she told him something important.

"Listen, you hardheaded boy. Respect yo elders and do what's right," she told him. "Don't you never, ever sass old people. Uh-uh! Treat them nice. Or they'll give you de eye and put de mout on you. Then you'll really be in a fix!" Little Muddy Waters just said, "Uh-huh."

Early the next morning he went on a walk. He came across Old Man Weava walking down the road with a pipe in his mouth. Weaving shrimp nets had been the man's job during his younger days. That's why he was called Weava. But his younger days had lo-o-o-ng gone. Now his face was as wrinkled as a hound dog's hide. And his eyes were glassy. And gray. Gray, just like the Spanish moss that hangs from St. Helena Island trees.

Old Man Weava always walked around with a little bag tied around his neck. That bag was filled with sulfur and garlic and bad smelling herbs. He said it was to keep away evil spirits. But it kept away anybody who came too close. Little Muddy Waters smelled the contents in that bag from afar off. He covered his nose. He smiled and said, "Good morning, Suh."

The old man studied the young boy up and down. He saw a space between the boy's two front teeth. So he said, "Boy, why you lie so much?"

"I don't tell lies," Little Muddy Waters answered. "I do not!"

"Yeah, you do, boy!" Weava shouted. "Why, yo teet tell de story." The old man chuckled. Then he added, "You got de Liar's Gap, Son! That's what yo teet say. Uh-huh!"

"They do not," Little Muddy Waters whispered. Then underneath his breath, he sassed, "Why you stink-stink old wrinkled bag of bones..."

"What you say?" Old Man Weava interrupted.

"Nothing," Little Muddy Waters lied. "I didn't say nothing atall." Well, that made the old man's blood run hot. He started closing one eye and pointed a finger in Little Muddy Waters' direction. He was getting ready to put mouth on the boy. To fix him. To make something happen to him that he'd never forget. Old Man Weava probably would've stopped if Little Muddy Waters had told the truth and said he was sorry. But Little Muddy Waters didn't remember Grandma Waters' good advice.

Weava started speaking in a whisper.

"So you don't know to respect yo elders, huh?" he said.

Then his voice got louder and louder.

"Why you ent nottin. You ent come from nottin. And if this day don't bring a good change in you, you ent gon mount to nottin. Mark my word!"

Then he slowly turned around and slowly walked away. Little Muddy Waters thought the old man had acted real strange. But he wasn't worried. He chuckled as he watched Old Man Weava leave.

"Change something about me?" he muttered silently. "I don't have to change nothing about me. You better change what you got in that bag, Old Man. Tee-hee-hee. Tee-hee-hee."

Then he turned around and skipped on home. When he got there, he curled up on his front porch and went to sleep.

But by and by, by and by, the old man's strange sounding words came true.
Cause there, right there on the front porch where that little boy had gone to
sleep curled up like a little ball—was a little ball of moss. Gray, just like the
old man's eyes.

Grandma Waters saw it when she came outside. She said, "Well, great day! My head da hurt and I need ta walk. This moss is just what I need to put in my shoes. To bring down my pressure."

So she put Little Muddy Waters...no, no...she put that ball of moss inside her shoes. To bring down her high blood pressure.

She walked off among the large oak trees and past the pretty St. Helena Island marshes. And she walked. And she walked. And she walked.

When she returned home, she felt a lot better. But Little
Muddy Waters—why that boy had almost had the life
   walked
      right
         out of him. Uh-uh-uh!

Grandma Waters took her shoes off and knocked them
against each other while she stood on the porch. The gray
Spanish moss fell onto the wooden floor before she padded
barefoot inside her house.

A few minutes later she heard a
scuffling noise on the porch. She
peeked out the front door and saw
Little Muddy Waters. He looked
tired-tired. Like he had been squeezed
into a very tight space. Like someone
had walked all over him. Like he had
done something he would never forget.

"Uh-uh-uh!" Grandma Waters said as
she rushed out to him. "Respect yo
elders and do what's right, Little Muddy
Waters," she said. "Now tell Grandma
all about what happened."

"Oh, Grandma," Little Muddy Waters sighed, "I hope you never put mouth on me. I'm gonna mind my manners. I'm gonna respect my elders. I'm gonna try to do what's right."

Grandma Waters hugged her grandson and patted his back. "That's so good to hear, Little Muddy Waters," she said. "But rememba now, I love you if you don't. And I love you if you do. Dat's da trut. Um-hm."

Respec Yo Eldas

(The Little Muddy Waters Song)

Verse I

Lyrics and Melody by Ronald Daise ©1997

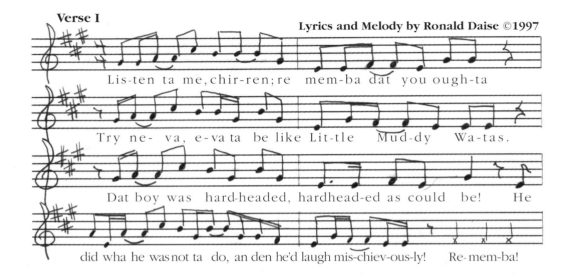

Lis-ten ta me, chir-ren; re mem-ba dat you ough-ta

Try ne- va, e-va ta be like Lit-tle Mud-dy Wa-tas.

Dat boy was hard-headed, hardhead-ed as could be! He

did wha he was not ta do, an den he'd laugh mis-chiev-ous-ly! Re-mem-ba!

Chorus

Res-pec yo el- das. Dats wha you ough- ta do!

Res-pec yo el-das, chir-ren; an den joy will come to you!

Res-pec yo el- das. Dats wha you ough- ta do!

Res-pec yo el-das, chir-ren; an den joy will come to you!

Verse II

Little Muddy Watas march(ed) right ta a bird nes,
Stuff(ed) his grandma's hair inside—now he knew dat wasn bes.
Dat wasn a good ting! It brought his grandma pain.
It gave her such a headache, cause dat boy forgot good mannas again.
Now listen

Chorus

Verse III

One day dat hardhead boy he sass(ed) an old-old man.
Talk(ed) back ta him so rudely. I jes cyan understan.
Dat old man got so mad he put 'de mout' on him.
Turn(ed) Muddy inta a ball a moss, an den dat boy's joy—it did end!
You hafta

Chorus

"Respec Yo Eldas," as performed by Ron and Natalie Daise, is available for purchase. To order, telephone 1-888-GOG-Song (464-7664).

BILL LITTELL

Ronald Daise, better known as "Mr. Ron" on Nickelodeon-TV's award-winning *Gullah Gullah Island,* is an actor, writer, singer, and songwriter. He is the author of *Reminiscences of Sea Island Heritage* (Sandlapper Publishing) and *De Gullah Storybook* (G.O.G. Enterprises). He also has written two Little Simon, Simon & Schuster sticker books, *Mr. Bradley's Day of Surprises* and *Let's Go to the Gullah Gullah Island Market.*

A storyteller through writing and music, Mr. Daise, along with his wife Natalie, has two recordings: *Sleep Tight, Lullabies & Night-Night Stories* and *Feel Like Journey On, Songs & Stories of Gullah Heritage for Children of All Ages.* The latter includes Mr. Daise's masterfully told "Little Muddy Waters" Gullah folktale.

Mr. Daise, a graduate of Hampton Institute, resides in Beaufort, South Carolina with his wife and their two children.

Barbara McArtor is an art teacher at St. Helena Elementary School, St. Helena, South Carolina, where she has inspired children to expand their creative abilities since she moved to Beaufort in 1987. Ms. McArtor works in other art disciplines including portrait painting, jewelry making, calligraphy, soft sculpture, and painting scenes on furniture. She also gives private art instruction. When she lived in Medina, Ohio, she helped found Mud Mothers, a studio and shop run cooperatively by area artists. Ms. McArtor is a graduate of Kent Sate University with a Bachelor of Science in Art Education.